The Egyptians

McLean County Unit #5
Carlock IMC - 105

The Egyptians

Pamela Odijk

Silver Burdett Press

McLean County Unit #5
Carlock IMC - 105

Acknowledgments

The author and publishers are grateful to the following for permission to reproduce copyright photographs and prints:

ANT/NHPA p. 13; The Mansell Collection p. 15; Ron Sheridan's Photo-Library pp. 12, 19 right, 21, 23, 28, 30, 31, 32, 35, 37, 38 and the cover photograph; Stock Photos pp. 9, 10, 27, 41; Werner Forman Archive pp. 14, 16, 18, 19 left, 20, 29.

While every care has been taken to trace and acknowledge copyright, the publishers tender their apologies for any accidental infringement where copyright has proved untraceable. They would be pleased to come to a suitable arrangement with the rightful owner in each case.

© Pamekla Odijk 1989

All rights reserved. No part of this publication
may be reproduced or transmitted, in any
form or by any means, without permission.

First published 1989 by
THE MACMILLAN COMPANY OF AUSTRALIA PTY LTD
107 Moray Street, South Melbourne 3205
6 Clarke Street, Crows Nest 2065

Adapted and first published in the United States in 1989
by Silver Burdett Press, Englewood Cliffs, N.J.

Library of Congress Cataloging-in-Publication Data

Odijk, Pamela, 1942–
    The Egyptians / Pamela Odijk.
        p.   cm.—(The Ancient world)
    Includes index.
    Summary: Discusses the civilization of ancient Egypt,
including the hunting, medicine, clothing, religion, laws, legends,
and recreation.
    1. Egypt—Civilization—To 332 B.C.—Juvenile literature.
    [1. Egypt—Civilization—To 332 B.C.]   I. Title.   II. Series:
Odijk, Pamela, 1942–   Ancient world.
DT61.035   1989
932—dc20   89-33858
ISBN 0-382-09886-2   CIP
                                                          AC

The Egyptians

Contents

The Egyptians: Timeline

Pre-Dynastic and archaic period.

2600 B.C.	2500	2400	2300	2200	2100

Old Kingdom: palettes and drawings found show battles and the lives of people. The drawings follow a sequence in the way a comic book is drawn. The great pyramids were built during this time including the step-pyramid, the three pyramids of Giza, the unfinished pyramid of Snofru and the great pyramid of Khufu (Cheops). The Sphinx was built from leftover stone from the pyramids.

Assyrians occupied Egypt.

1600	1500	1400	1300	1200	1100	1000	900	800	700	600	500

New Kingdom: period of greatness and power but the civilization eventually declined and disintegrated. Pyramids ceased to be used as royal tombs. A new kind of monument temple began to be built. Ordinary people had small pyramids built on their tombs. Buildings constructed at this time were: temples at Luxor, Karnak, the great temple of Seti I at Abydos, the Nubian rocks temple of Rameses II at Abu Simbel.
Then the power of the pharaohs began to decrease and invasion of Egypt occurred which stopped the development of art.

Persian conquest of Egypt.

Middle Kingdom: Egyptian culture rose to great heights, but also suffered great turmoil. The country was invaded. Social revolution and economic decline happened at this time. Huge monuments and tombs could no longer be afforded. Models, often made of wood and painted, were put in tombs instead of full-sized articles. Forts were built in southern Egypt. Smaller pyramids were built. In middle Egypt, rock-cut tombs of nobles were built. Art became more uniform. Tomb paintings showed more scenes from everyday life. Goldsmiths excelled in their craft.

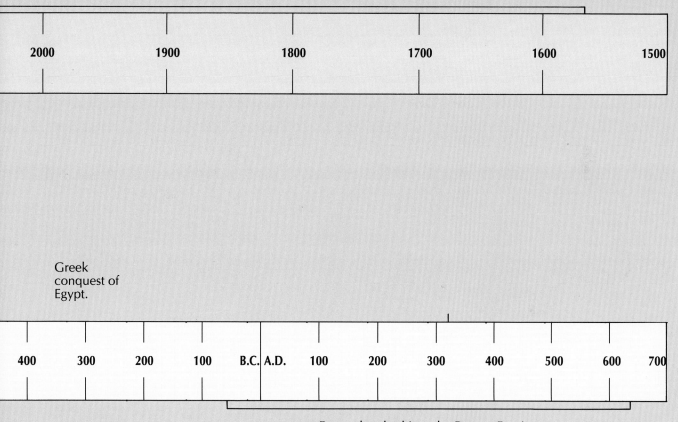

2000   1900   1800   1700   1600   1500

Greek
conquest of
Egypt.

400   300   200   100   B.C. A.D.   100   200   300   400   500   600   700

Egypt absorbed into the Roman Empire.

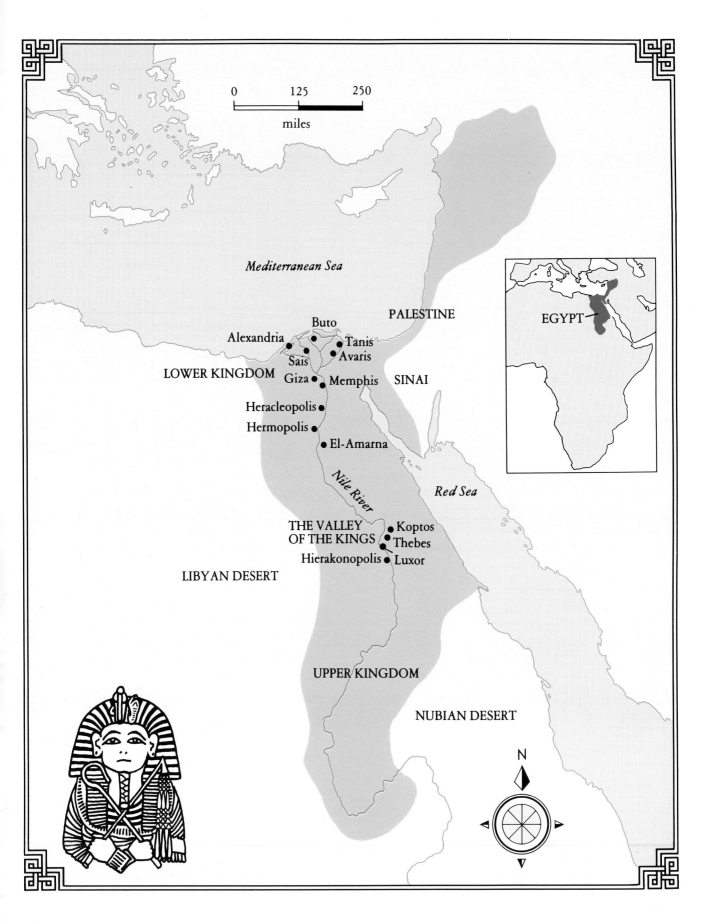

Mediterranean Sea

PALESTINE

Buto

Alexandria

Tanis

Avaris

Sais

LOWER KINGDOM

Giza

Memphis

SINAI

Heracleopolis

Hermopolis

El-Amarna

Nile River

Red Sea

THE VALLEY
OF THE KINGS

Koptos

Thebes

Hierakonopolis

Luxor

LIBYAN DESERT

UPPER KINGDOM

NUBIAN DESERT

EGYPT

N

The Egyptians: Introduction

The early Egyptians were the first people to live in the area through which the longest river in the world, the Nile, flows. They were among the first people to change from a food-gathering way of life to a food-producing way of life. Egyptians depended upon the cycles of nature, particularly the regular yearly flooding of the Nile to grow and harvest their crops and graze their animals successfully. This was because they lived in a desert environment. The flooding of the Nile gave them water for irrigation and deposited rich **silt** on the land.

The Egyptians were generally a peaceful and practical people who accepted the world as it was and made the best possible use of all they found. They spent time perfecting their arts and crafts and were excellent engineers and builders. Egyptian writing, called **hieroglyphics**, was already advanced by 3100 B.C. Being great traders, the Egyptians once controlled the trade routes of the Near East.

From time to time the breakdown of central government led to civil wars and disrupted the early Egyptian way of life, but leaders and rulers always sought to restore unity and peace. Eventually the Egyptians established professional armies to defend the country and people. The **pharaoh**, who was also king and a god to the people, was the supreme ruler.

Avenue of Ram-headed Sphinxes at the Karnak Temple in Luxor, Egypt.

Water bearers, River Nile, Egypt. The ancient Egyptians were dependent on the annual flooding of the Nile for their livelihood.

The progressive life of the Egyptians ended after twenty-two centuries in about 525 B.C., when the Persians, followed by the Greeks and the Romans, gained control of Egypt.

The glory and serenity of the Egyptian civilization can be seen in the pyramids, while its power and wealth can be seen in the temples at Thebes.

Egypt's history is usually divided into the following periods:

Name	Dates	What Happened
Pre-Dynastic and Archaic	Era predating 2600 B.C.	Mesopotamian settlers brought irrigation techniques to the Nile Valley.
Old Kingdom	2600-2100 B.C.	Twenty pyramids and the **Sphinx** were built during this time. The capital was Memphis.
Middle Kingdom	2100-1567 B.C.	Egyptian culture rose to great heights but also suffered great turmoil, and the country was invaded.
New Kingdom	1567-1085 B.C.	Initially great and powerful but later declined and disintegrated. The capital was at Thebes.

The Importance of Landforms and Climate

The landforms and climate of any area determine, to a large extent, how people live, what kinds of crops can be grown and where, and what kinds of animals can be kept.

Landforms

For the Egyptians, the Nile River dominated their land, winding its way for a total length of 4,150 miles (6,670 kilometers) and for about 720 miles (1,200 kilometers) from the lake now called Lake Nasser to the city of Cairo. This river, rising and falling regularly, would flood the valley from July to September and return to its normal level in October each year. The planting and harvesting would be organized around the flood cycle of the Nile. The floodwaters would bring with them a rich silt, washed down from the faraway hills, which would spread over the valley providing fertile soil in which crops grew very well.

On both sides the fertile, narrow valley was hemmed in by desert with high mountains in the southwest and a narrow coastal plain, none of which were suitable for growing crops or

Apart from the fertile Nile Valley, the rest of ancient Egypt was barren desert, useless for growing crops and raising animals.

raising animals. Most people lived in the Nile Valley.

Here, on each side, the Egyptians were protected from invaders by vast expanses of desert, which allowed them to live a peaceful and somewhat isolated existence. As a result Egyptian tools and ways of doing things were quite different from those of other people in the ancient world.

Climate

Egypt, lying in the desert belt, receives almost no rain. The days are very hot and the nights very cold. Between March and June, desert **cyclones** occur, bringing hot, dry winds which often reach gale force.

Winter lasts from November to March, bringing cool and mild days, while the hottest part of the year is from May to September.

The rains come mainly in the winter, and more rain falls in the north than in the south. Alexandria's rainfall is about 1/2 inch (17 millimeters) each year; at Cairo and along the Red Sea there is hardly any rain at all.

All of these conditions determine the kinds of crops that can be grown and what kinds of animals can be raised, as they, too, must be able to survive.

Natural Plants, Animals, and Birds

Plants that grow naturally in the area, and animals and birds that live upon the land and among the people also are important. The Egyptians learned to use trees and plants that grew naturally and to plant others that would grow with them. By observing animals in the wild, the Egyptians learned how to catch and domesticate them.

Plants

In the lower Nile Valley grew tall **papyrus** reeds from which the Egyptians learned to make paper and other items. Here also grew over one hundred different kinds of grasses, including reeds and bamboo. Tamarisk, acacia, and some leafless trees grew in drier areas, along with thorny shrubs, succulent plants, and herbs. Lotus, date palms, and African fan palms grew along the Nile.

Animals and Birds

Animals found in Egypt in early times included hippopotamuses, giraffes, rodents (including the large and strong pharaoh rat), and the striped Egyptian mongoose. Egypt has always had many birds. Other birds passed through Egypt as they migrated to the northern and southern summers. Among the most famous birds of early Egypt were the golden eagles, lanner falcons, great egrets, herons and sacred ibis, ostriches, and many varieties of desert birds.

Among the creatures to be feared were poisonous snakes, scorpions, and crocodiles. Locusts and other insects often reached plague proportions and ate the crops.

The Nile always had a plentiful supply of fish. Many tomb paintings show the variety of sea life and the pleasures of fishing.

Opposite: the River Nile at Aswan and the ruins of the Temple on Elephantine Island. Varieties of palm trees still grow on the banks of the Nile.

Below: hippopotamuses were found in ancient Egypt.

Crops, Herds, and Hunting

The fertile soil of the Nile Valley with its large areas of farmland, regular rainfall, and warm climate provided ideal conditions for the Egyptians to become expert farmers. The towns were the market places for produce. The grand **vizier**, assisted by a chief of the fields and a master of **largesse**, who looked after livestock, controlled Egyptian agriculture. The land was divided into estates. A landlord controlled each estate and the **tenant farmers** who worked on it. Some of these landlords were very wealthy.

Much of our knowledge of the ancient Egyptians comes from artifacts and paintings found by archaeologists. This painting from the tomb of Nakht in Thebes shows grapes being crushed and made into wine.

Crops

Land was irrigated by diverting the waters of the Nile into canals, and using **shadufs** to scoop up the water. Seed was lent to the tenant farmers, along with animals such as oxen and asses to pull the plows and to carry heavy loads. Fields were plowed once or twice. Remaining clods of earth were then broken up by men wielding hoes. When the seed was sown, animals were used again to tread the seed well into the soil. Crops such as **emmer**, barley, and **flax** (used to make linen) were grown, along with **lentils**, onions, and beans. In very early Egypt, millet is thought to have been the main crop.

Crops of grain were harvested using sickles made of sharp flint blades in long handles. To thresh out the grain, the collected harvest was placed on a hard surface and animals trampled

on it. It was then sifted by tossing it into the air so the chaff would blow away, leaving the grain to fall to the ground. The grain was then stored in silos (underground pits).

Herds

After crops were harvested, farm animals and herds of sheep, cattle, goats, and pigs were sent in to graze on the stubble. Cattle and goats were raised both for meat and milk. Barbary, black, piebald, and white sheep were raised, as well as sheep with coarse coats (called kempy coats), and special sheep with fat, heavy tails.

From pictures on **artifacts**, utensils, statues, and tombs and from remains of animals' bones we know that the Egyptians kept draft animals long before written records were kept. Don-

keys were being used in Egypt before 3500 B.C. and wheeled vehicles were in use by 1600 B.C. People were riding horses by 1345 B.C. The Egyptians also bred special dogs for hunting.

Hunting

Hunters were a special class of persons, who either hunted alone or assisted nobles with hunting. Animals hunted included gazelle, antelopes, stag, wild oxen, hares, ostriches (for their plumes), foxes, jackals, wolves, hyenas, and leopards. Nets, nooses, and arrows were used to hunt these animals.

An Egyptian shaduf is used for scooping up water from man-made canals and from the Nile. This irrigation system was invented by the ancient Egyptians and is still used in Egypt today as shown here.

How Families Lived

Egyptians believed that conditions on earth could not be changed and that the kind of family one was born into had to be accepted. Poverty had to be humbly endured. This belief changed, however, with the New Kingdom (1567–1085 B.C.), when people found it possible to improve their social position. Some people from humble origins even gained positions of prominence. Society in Egypt was organized in a hierarchy as described in the table below.

Egyptian law ensured that women and men had equal rights, independence, and equal status. Both worked in all sections of the economy and took part in public life. Boys and girls in families were treated equally.

Ruler Pharaoh (King).
Officials Administrators, scribes, priests, and nobles.
Middle Class Merchants.
Working People Farmers, harvesters, herders, artisans and craftspeople in workshops, **(including** fishermen, boat builders, dancers, house workers, and homemakers. **Peasants)**
Slaves and Servants Worked for all the above.

Remains of furniture found in the Giza tomb of Hetepheres I, the chief queen of Snofru and the mother of Khufu. This furniture is from the Old Kingdom. It shows what the furniture of the pharaohs was like, as they had objects of everyday use buried with them in their tombs for use in the afterlife.

Houses

Stone and mud bricks made of soil from the river banks were used as building materials. Houses in towns and villages were set out in a square or rectangle. Excavations suggest that the earliest furniture was brick platforms, which served as chairs, tables, and beds, made comfortable by coverings of animal skins. Murals painted on the walls of houses and floors represented gardens and pools.

Colors used in decorating included brilliant yellow, **terracotta**, gray, and black. Later furniture ranged from simple benches in poorer homes to beautiful chairs, tables, and beds in the wealthier family homes. Dating back to the third **millennium** B.C., Egyptians wove carpets from linen and decorated them with colored pieces of wool. Rich Egyptians could afford luxurious villas with large, shady gardens.

Education

Egyptian boys and girls were treated equally and given the kind of education best suited to their future adult roles. Children of wealthier families had more privileges than poorer children. Formal education was usually controlled by the priests. Children started school at the age of 5 and completed it at 16 or 17. From the age of 13 or 14, boys were given special training, or they could enter a temple college and train to become a priest or **scribe**. Science, medicine, and mathematics were taught in formal schools. Vocational skills, such as building and architecture, engineering, domestic arts, child-rearing, and sculpture, were taught outside the formal schools.

Layout of a wealthier Egyptian house.

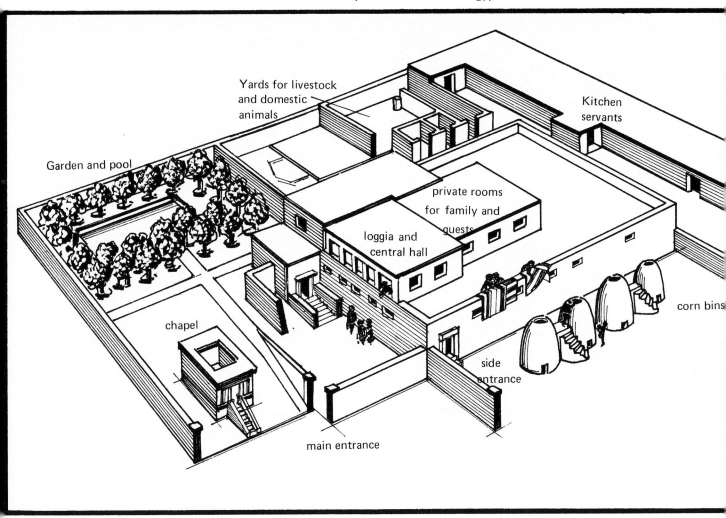

Yards for livestock and domestic animals

Kitchen servants

Garden and pool

private rooms for family and guests

loggia and central hall

corn bins

chapel

side entrance

main entrance

Food, Medicine, and Clothes

Food

The Egyptians had an abundant supply of food. Flour was ground from grain and made into bread. Brewing and baking were skills known to the Egyptians, who made over fifty different kinds of bread using methods not very different from those used today. Other cooking was done over open fires or roasting pits.

Lentils were dried and made into soups, stews, and cakes. In both the towns and country villages, vegetable gardens were cultivated to produce asparagus, cabbages, chards, watermelons, celery, cucumbers, lettuce, onions, peas, radishes, and grapes.

Detail from a tomb painting showing the plucking and preparation of poultry.

Animals were kept for meat and milk. Poultry, fruit, and fish were plentiful. Honey was used for sweetening.

Food was served from baked-clay dishes and bowls, and was eaten with spoons or with fingers. Carving knives were made from flints set into wooden handles, but only the wealthy had knives for eating.

Servants and slaves helped prepare, cook, and serve foods. In Egypt, as with all ancient civilizations, the selection, preparation, and enjoyment of food was very important. Food offerings were made to the dead.

Medicine

Egyptians had extensive medical knowledge. **Mummies**, some of which have survived to this day, demonstrated the Egyptians' knowledge of the preservative properties of the herbs they used in the **embalming** process. Egyptian papyri dating from 1600 B.C. contain a number of descriptions about the structure and function of the human body. By 1500 B.C., Egyptian doctors were very much aware of the importance of the human heart. Other medical records from ancient Egypt include formulas used by practicing doctors and over 260 prescriptions, including cures for animal stings. Also, special prayers, spells, and incantations were believed to help cure diseases.

Clothes

By carefully studying ancient paintings and sculpture, we can discover what Egyptian clothes looked like. Papyrus documents also tell us about materials used and what they were made from.

Both sexes wore many ornaments, ranging from pendants, bracelets, anklets, **amulets**, and bangles to ribbons and garlands for poorer people. A particularly common piece of jewelry was the usekh, a necklace made of many strands, and pendants which covered the wearer from neck to waist. Wigs were also worn by both sexes for ornament and as protection from the sun. Women wore cosmetics for the same reasons. Men were smooth-shaven. Both men and women wore sandals or went barefoot.

Egyptians could not dye clothes very well, because garments needed to be washed frequently. For special occasions, fabrics were dyed yellow, blue, green, or red. Some had colored patterns. Tapestry and embroidery seem to have been used only on garments belonging to the king. Clothing became more elaborate during the period of the New Kingdom.

Children are depicted without clothes and with shaven heads, except for one lock of hair called the "lock of youth," which hung down one side of the head.

This detail from the Book of the Dead shows clothes worn by ancient Egyptian men and women.

An ivory comb from the Old Kingdom.

Linen was the most common material. It was woven from fibers of the flax plant. Linen was light and easy to wash. Wool was not used extensively for clothing, although heavy **mantles** were worn by men and women in colder weather. Silk and cotton were not known in early times.

Clothing was draped, pleated, and wrapped around the body. Men wore loin cloths and kilts of varying lengths, which were wrapped and tied in front. In later times men wore a simple square shirt with holes for the arms and head, while women wore long linen skirts.

Religion and Rituals of the Egyptians

The Egyptians had many gods. Each god had many forms and powers. Temples were built to these gods, and the gods were believed to live in the temples in the form of a statue. Each day the god's shrine would be opened, the statue dressed and given offerings of food and drink.

The pharaoh was believed to be the son of the sun god, Amon, also known as Re. The god of the afterlife was Osiris who, it was believed, dwelled in the dead pharaoh and who, in turn, passed his powers on to his son.

Chapel of the Tomb of Merye-hufer Qar, Giza.

Festivals

There were many religious festivals, most of which centered on the annual flooding on the Nile and the life-giving force of the sun. There were festivals for celebrating the birth, death, and crowning of the pharaoh as well as the seasons and their life-giving activities. There were also festivals dedicated to particular gods and goddesses, such as the Festival of Min (the god of fertility), celebrated during the harvest. At this festival the pharaoh and his queen performed a special marriage ritual. Festivals featured sacrificial offerings, feasting, drinking, and dancing. There were festivals devoted to specials days, such as the New Year and the first day of each month.

Anubis the embalmer.

Some Egyptian Gods and Goddesses

Name	Other Names	What the God Represented	Usual Symbol
Amon	Amen, Ammon, Amun	King of gods, patron of the pharaohs, identified with the sun god Re as Ammon-Re.	Male figure with a ram's head.
Anubis	Anpu	God of the dead.	Black jackal or male figure with a dog's head.
Aton	Aten	Sun at its zenith, a form of the sun god Re.	A red solar disk with rays ending in hands.
Atum	Tem, Tum	Creator of gods.	Old bearded man wearing a double crown.
Bast	Bastet, Ubasti	Goddess of music and dance.	Cat or a woman with a cat's head.
Bes	Bisu	Protector of the royal house, protector and bringer of peace for the dead.	Dwarf with a large head, large eyes, protruding tongue, bowlegs, and bush tail.

Name	Other Names	What the God Represented	Usual Symbol
Buto	Edjo, Udjo, Wadjet, Wadjit	Defender of the king, sun's burning heat.	Female figure wearing the red crown of Lower Egypt.
Geb	Keb, Seb	God of the earth.	Goose or male figure with the head of a goose.
Hathor	Athyr	Originally personification of the sky, protector of women, goddess of love and joy.	Cow or goddess with a cow's head or female goddess with horns or cow's ears.
Horus	Hor	Originally god of Lower Egypt but later god of the reigning king.	Falcon or male figure with a falcon's head.
Isis	Aset, Eset	Queen of the gods. Sister-wife of Osiris.	Female figure with headdress and a throne.
Ma'at	Mayet	Goddess of law, truth, and justice.	Female figure with an ostrich feather on her head, standing or sitting on her heels.
Min		God of fertility and harvest, and the protector of desert travelers.	Bearded man with two tall plumes on his gown and holding a flail or thunderbolt in his right hand.
Mut		Vulture goddess; great and divine mother, wife of Amon.	Female figure with vulture headdress.
Nekhbet	Nekhebet	Protectress of childbirth.	Woman or vulture wearing white crown of Upper Egypt.
Nut	Neuth, Nuit	Goddess of the sky, protectress of the dead.	Female figure arched over Shu with a water pot on her head.
Osiris	Usire	Originally fertility god, later ruled with Re, god of the afterlife.	Dead king in mummy wrappings with a crown. Holds a crook or flail.
Ptah	Phthah	Creator of things, patron of artists and metal workers.	Mummified man with a shaven head. Holds a scepter.
Re	Phra, Ra	Sun god, king of gods, and father of mankind.	Man with a falcon head crowned with the sun disk. Holds an ankh (cross) and scepter.
Sebek	Sebeq, Sobk, Suchos	Protector of reptiles and patron of kings, water god.	Crocodile or man with a crocodile's head wearing a solar disk.
Sekhmet	Sekhet	Warlike solar goddess.	Lioness or woman with a lion's head.

Name	Other Names	What the God Represented	Usual Symbol
Seth	Set, Setekh, Setesh	Partner or rival of Horus, storm god.	Composite creature with a greyhound's body, slanting eyes, and forked tail.
Shu		God of light and air, the divine intelligence.	Male figure with an ostrich's figure on his head.
Thoth	Djhowtey	Moon god, inventor of hieroglyphic writing and the god of learning.	Male figure with an ibis's head on which was a moon crescent and a disk.

Life After Death

The Egyptians believed that life on earth was only a part of an individual's total life. After an earthly death, a person was believed to enter an afterlife of eternity. Everything that might have been required in the afterlife was buried with the person. Tombs of the pharaohs in the pyramids contained great treasures, along with useful items such as furniture and food. Animals, family members, and slaves were killed and buried with the pharaoh, in early times, so that they could serve him in his afterlife. Ordinary people and poor people had much less elaborate burials and funerals.

To preserve the body in death, the Egyptians developed and used embalming techniques called mummification. This procedure involved removing the body's organs and then using natron (a form of sodium) to dry out the body's tissues. The body was then stuffed with resins and preserving oils, wrapped in specially prepared strips of linen and placed first in a coffin and then in a tomb.

Egyptians believed that after death the god Osiris and forty-two judges weighed the dead person's heart on a scale and balanced it against a feather to see if it was heavy with sin. Incantations from the Book of the Dead could be used to gain entrance into the afterlife.

Statue of Sekhmet, the warlike solar goddess, found at Thebes.

Obeying the Law

Egyptian law was closely tied to religion. The Egyptians believed in the divine pharaoh who ruled supreme. From the time of the Old Kingdom, some of the power was delegated to others such as the vizier, who oversaw every aspect of government. The vizier also tried law cases and acted as custodian of all legal documents.

In Egyptian law great emphasis was placed on the rights of the individual, with men and women having equal rights. The poor and the wealthy were equal before the law and even slaves had rights. When the Greeks and Romans controlled Egypt in later times, they influenced Egyptian law and in turn were influenced by these laws.

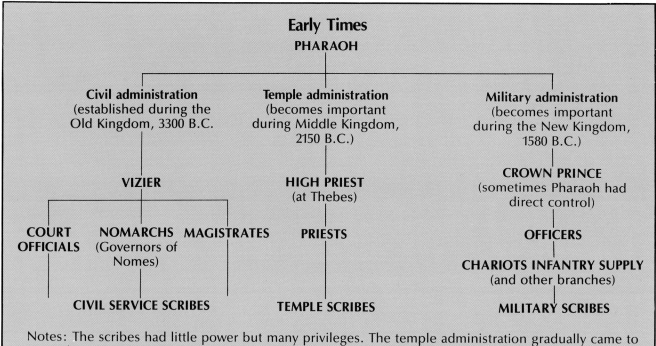

Early Times

PHARAOH

Civil administration (established during the Old Kingdom, 3300 B.C.

Temple administration (becomes important during Middle Kingdom, 2150 B.C.)

Military administration (becomes important during the New Kingdom, 1580 B.C.)

VIZIER

HIGH PRIEST (at Thebes)

CROWN PRINCE (sometimes Pharaoh had direct control)

COURT OFFICIALS **NOMARCHS** (Governors of Nomes) **MAGISTRATES**

PRIESTS

OFFICERS

CHARIOTS INFANTRY SUPPLY (and other branches)

CIVIL SERVICE SCRIBES

TEMPLE SCRIBES

MILITARY SCRIBES

Notes: The scribes had little power but many privileges. The temple administration gradually came to control more and more of the land: 15 percent in 1200 B.C., and 30 percent by 1085 B.C.

Property laws

Every person, including slaves, could own and dispose of property. Originally, records of all property ownership were recorded by scribes at one central location. Later, people could have deeds drawn up to show ownership.

Marriage laws

Men and women had equal rights in marriage, with a certain percentage of property being shared as marriage property. All other property belonged to the individual. Slaves who married free people became free.

Divorce laws

Divorce became part of Egyptian law from 1085 to 332 B.C.

Inheritance

Children inherited the property of their parents, with the exception of the shared marriage property. Usually the eldest son inherited the family property, but other arrangements could be made by the parents if they had a special document drawn up, similar to a will.

Children were expected to pay for their parents' funerals and to maintain the tombs after death.

People would appear before a court on their own behalf.

Courts

People spoke before the court on their own behalf, presented any documents as evidence, and then spoke again. They could also call witnesses. When all of the evidence was recorded, the judge would make a decision.

Minor cases were judged by officials, and more important cases were heard by the vizier. In very important cases, the pharaoh would be the judge or would appoint a special judge or judges.

Punishments

Punishments set by the courts were very severe. They included being beaten, locked up, and sometimes having a limb cut off.

Writing It Down: Recording Things

The first Egyptian writing was done on stone. When the Greeks entered Egypt and saw this writing carved into the stone temples and monuments, they called it **hieroglyphics** (sacred writing). The Egyptians also wrote on a type of paper which was made from the papyrus reeds that grew along the banks of the Nile. Writing on papyrus was done with a reed pen dipped in an ink made from vegetable gum, soot, and water. Rolls of papyri were often inscribed and hung in Egyptian temples, and because they could be rolled up and moved, they were used as portable inscriptions.

For legal documents and everyday records, the Egyptians invented a simpler version of hieroglyphics called **demotic script**, which was used from about 660 B.C. onward. Egyptian writing is generally done from right to left.

In 1798, when Napoleon landed in Egypt with his army and scholars, he discovered a large stone, called the **Rosetta Stone**, on which examples of hieroglyphics, demotic script, and Greek appeared. French professor Jean-Francois Champollion spent ten years studying this stone and deciphering Egyptian writing. Now, surviving documents could be read. However, many important documents about ancient Egypt and its people have not survived.

Only fragments of one important document listing the kings of Egypt have survived, and they are kept at the Museo Egizio in Turin, Italy.

Annals

From about 3000 B.C. onward, each year was named after major events. These events were recorded along with the height of the Nile flood for each year and written in a register. These records became known as **annals**. Later, kings would consult these annals to see if certain events had happened previously. Most of these annals have been lost too. Only fragments of annals from 3000 to 2345 B.C. have survived.

Numbers

The Egyptians devised a way of recording numbers. But the only knowledge we have of Egyptian mathematics is contained in two papyri at present held in the Soviet Union and Great Britain.

Opposite: the bird god at Luxor. Hieroglyphics were carved on the wall by the ancient Egyptians.

Means Available for Recording

These could be combined to make new words.

- **Pictograms** pictures of objects.
- **Ideograms** an extension of pictograms, where simple signs and characters stood for ideas or objects. (The Chinese and Japanese use ideograms.)
- **Phonograms** in which characters stand for sounds and
- **Alphabetic letters**

Recording Time

The Egyptians were the first to devise an accurate calendar of 365 days that was compatible with the seasons. Their calendar consisted of twelve months of thirty days, with five days at the end of each year belonging to no month. Originally the months were numbered, but from the third century B.C. onward they were named for festivals, and the years were named for major events. The only record of time greater than a year was the reign of a king.

Seasons

Each year had three seasons: Inundation, when the Nile flooded the land; Going Forth, when the Nile returned to normal and planting of crops began; and Deficiency, when the harvest occurred and the Nile was at its lowest.

Clocks

The Egyptians used sundials to measure time during the daylight hours. The earliest known sundial is an Egyptian shadow clock dating from the eighth century B.C. Clocks of this kind are still used in parts of Egypt.

At night, water clocks were used. These clocks were vessels or buckets filled with water

Water clock from Karnak Temple, dated 1415 B.C.

with a small hole in the bottom. The time was marked on a scale inside the bucket. The Greeks later adopted this invention.

Weights and Measures

Egyptian weights were based on a unit called a kite.

    10 kites = 1 deben
    10 debens = 1 sep

A kite varied from .16 ounce (4.5 grams) to 1.06 ounces (29.9 grams) over the centuries of Egyptian history.

Liquid measures from large to small were ro, hin, and hekat.

Cubit

The cubit was an Egyptian standard measure based on the length of the arm from the elbow to the extended fingertips.

    1 digit = 1 finger's length
    28 digits = 1 Royal cubit
    (Royal cubit = 20.62 inches or 524 centimeters)
    4 digits = 1 palm
    12 digits or 3 palms = 1 small span
    16 digits or 4 palms = 1 t'ser
    24 digits or 6 palms = 1 small cubit.

Digits were further subdivided. The Great Pyramid of Giza was built using this system of measure.

Egyptian shadow clock.

Egyptian Legends

There were various kinds of Egyptian legends. Some were religious tales concerning the gods and their spirit and animal forms, while others were about mortals. Prose and poetry were usually reserved for praising gods, while only prose was used for secular (nonreligious) tales.

The oldest tales still existing from Egypt were written on papyrus at about the end of the second millennium B.C.

In later times the Greeks were fascinated by the Egyptian myths and legends and wrote about them.

Some Popular Legends That Have Survived

King (Cheops) Khufu and the Magician: about ancient kings.

The Shipwrecked Sailor: about a castaway on an island who is entertained by a monster serpent.

Tale of Two Brothers: about a good young man accused of a misdeed by his older brother.

The Contendings of Horus and Seth: a comic story about the gods.

The Tale of the Eloquent Peasant: about a peasant whose pleasant pleadings gain him justice.

The Report of Wenamun: describes the troubles of an official sent to Phoenicia to buy timber.

The Story of Sinuhe: about an official in exile who receives the pharaoh's pardon and returns home.

The Pyramid Texts: texts found on the inside walls of the pyramids are magical texts to assure survival of the king's soul. These texts became available to nobles in the Middle Kingdom (coffin texts) and to commoners later (Book of the Dead).

Pyramid texts inscribed on the inside walls of the Pyramid of Unas, Saqqara, from the Old Kingdom.

Art and Architecture

The great Egyptian pyramids and temples were built of stone. The stone was shaped by highly skilled stonemasons. The stones were pulled to their location on rollers, and then raised by peasants and slaves using ramps and levers. Well-qualified and imaginative architects designed these magnificent structures and supervised their construction. These pyramids served as elaborate tombs for the pharaohs. They also remind us that the Egyptians did not invent machines but used imaginatively nature's materials and human labor.

Egyptian art was designed to serve the interests of religion and to provide beautiful houses for the upper class. Much art was designed to portray life after death for a country gentleman. The images of life as represented in Egyptian art are almost unchanging over time.

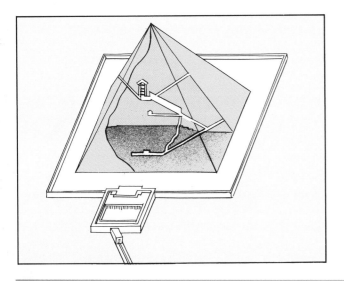

Opposite: the gold mask of Tutankhamon.

Left: the inner tombs of a pyramid.

Below: the pyramids at Giza.

Colors used in Egyptian art and architecture were obtained from colored earth. Splashes of primary colors, yellow, terracotta, gray, and black were used for contrast. By 1500 B.C. dyes such as **indigo** and **madder** were imported, and a gum was being manufactured from the acacia tree and used extensively. Egyptians copied motifs and designs from forms appearing in nature, such as lotus buds and flowers, papyri reeds, palm trees, animals, and birds. Natural colors were preferred.

Egyptian art and architecture evolved and changed. The stages of evolution correspond to recognized historical periods as shown on the next page.

The Sphinx at Giza.

Historic Period	Art and Architecture
Pre-Dynastic	From Upper Egypt, animal, bird, and geometric shapes have been found on cream and red clay vessels. Some stone vases were made very large, hollowed out of stone and shaped like frogs, birds, and hippopotomuses. Cosmetic palettes, some shaped like turtles, were found in tombs from this time. Items made of copper and gold were found. Rock drawings from this time show boats and animals. Most drawings show animals and people in profile, while torsos of people are shown in front view. Small stone and clay figurines have been found dating from this time.
Old Kingdom	Throughout Egyptian history, temples (houses of the gods) and kings' tombs (eternal houses for the body and soul) were built of stone. Towns, including palaces, shops, and houses, were built of mud brick. The great pyramids were built during this time, including the step pyramid and the three pyramids of Giza. The sphinx was built from bedrock and blocks added to model the lion's head, which resembled the ruler Khafre. Lesser tombs were also built of mud brick with different types of experimental arches and vaults. These tombs were often decorated with pictures of the dead person's family. Many buildings had decorative columns and **friezes**. Richly carved furniture of ebony and wood overlaid with gold was found in tombs built during this time, together with ornaments and personal jewelry.
	Palettes and drawings showing battles and the lives of people have been found. The drawings follow a sequence in the way a comic book is drawn. In sculpture and painting, figures became more lifelike and workers were shown with their tools of trade.
Middle Kingdom	Smaller pyramids were built but in a different style; one has a porch of many columns on all sides of the pyramid. Rock-cut tombs were also used for nobles. Forts were built in southern Egypt to guard the frontier. Tomb paintings showed more scenes from everyday life. Goldsmiths excelled at their craft. Models of painted wood showing various activities, such as baking bread and butchering cattle, were put in the tomb to assure continuation of such activities in the afterlife.
New Kingdom	The arts again flourished, and buildings and monuments were constructed on a grand scale. Kings, queens, and nobles were buried in rock-cut tombs. The best examples of art in this period come from the Tomb of Tutankhamon. Human figures were depicted as being more slender and graceful, and both movements and perspective become standardized.
	A new kind of momumental temple began to be built. These include the great temples at Karnak, at Luxor, and the Nubian rock temple of Rameses II at Abu Simbel.
	Then the power of the pharaohs began to decrease. Frequent invasions led to a decline in the development of art.

Going Places: Transportation, Exploration, and Communication

The ancient Egyptians sailed their boats along the Nile as far as where Khartoum now stands, and along the Blue Nile to Lake Tana. They showed less interest in the White Nile and the source of the Nile, perhaps assuming that the existence of the Nile was simply the work of the gods. Over time, however, the Egyptians became great travelers and traders, covering much of the Mediterranean. The Red Sea was an important commercial route by 2000 B.C. and was later used as a route to India. Ship canals were dug between the Nile and the Red Sea but were later abandoned.

Ships

The earliest ships were made from bundles of reeds lashed together and coated with **pitch**, but the Egyptians developed large wooden seagoing vessels by 3000 B.C. These large ships had a huge rectangular sail made of linen. These ships could sail across the wind and before the wind. Oars were used to propel the ship against the wind. The vessel was steered by two huge parallel oars.

An Egyptian two-wheeled chariot as shown on tomb paintings.

Today, the Egyptians navigate their sailing vessels along the Nile as did the ancient Egyptians.

When Queen Hatshepsut ruled Egypt, she began a great period of prosperity from about 1503 B.C. She believed trade was more important to a country than military exploits, and she sent a famous trading expedition to the land of Punt.

Trade was conducted by barter (the exchange of goods). Egyptians did not use money as we know it.

Roads

The Egyptians built the first roads, which provided a surface along which to haul the huge stones used to construct their temples and pyramids. The roads leading to the temples were subsequently paved. Wheeled vehicles did not appear on Egyptian roads until about 1600 B.C., when lightweight **chariots** with spoked wheels were introduced. Pack animals were used for transportation, and there is evidence that people were riding horses in Egypt about 1345 B.C..

Maps

Mapping skills were developed in ancient Egypt and Babylon. Land drawings have been found in early tombs. The Egyptians made surveys and **plats** (plans or maps) as soon as settlements were established in the fertile areas of the Nile Valley. Later, plats were also made for canals, roads, and temples.

Music, Dancing, and Recreation

In all ancient civilizations, music and dancing were inseparable parts of religion and worship, which dominated peoples' lives. Religious festivals often revolved around the seasons, which in turn controlled the crops and the activities of farming people.

The harp was played mostly by women and used in secular entertainment, though it was also used for religious and sacred purposes.

Singers

Singers played a very important role in Egyptian music. They developed a special technique called **chironomy** to direct the instrumentalists. There was no system of music notation in ancient times.

Dancers

Dancers performed in religious and ceremonial dances, often wearing masks that represented an animal or a god. These dances were very complicated and could be performed only by people who had been specially trained.

Secular dances were performed purely for entertainment. One of the earliest written documents about dancing comes from Egypt and describes dancers (including pygmy dancers) brought from Africa to perform. Egyptians also had performing acrobatic dancers.

Figures of dancers were painted on the insides of tombs, perhaps with the belief that they would entertain the dead.

Other Recreations

Board games have been found in Egyptian tombs. Also, various kinds of dice and knuckle bones have been found. It is not known exactly how these games were played.

Wrestling, swimming, and a type of water fencing were also popular. Dolls, leather balls, and toy animals were used by children, and tomb paintings show pictures of children playing games and dancing. Religious and military processions were partly entertainment and partly spectacle.

Egyptian Musical Instruments		
Group Name	**How Instrument Made Sound**	**Examples**
Idiophones	Sound made by instrument resonating as a whole.	Cymbals
Aerophones	Sound resonates on a column of blown air.	Pipes
Chordophones	Sound resonates when strings are plucked.	Harp, Lyre, Lute
Membranophones	Sound resonates when stretched skins are struck.	Drum
Rattles	Sound made when instrument is shaken.	Sistrum, Timbrel

Wars and Battles

The ancient Egyptians were peaceful people who lived an isolated existence. In the days of the Old Kingdom (2600–2200 B.C.), there was no regular army. During the Middle Kingdom (2000–1800 B.C.), the pharaohs created and trained a permanent army because Egypt lacked many raw materials. Sometimes these materials had to be procured by force. When Egypt grew into a prosperous country, it also needed to be defended by powerful and loyal armies.

The Egyptian Army

The Egyptian army was led by the pharaoh in his royal chariot, followed by other war chariots. Each chariot carried two men: one to fight and one to drive the chariot. Behind the chariots followed the armed foot soldiers. Foot soldiers did not wear **armor**. Peasants were often forced to serve as soldiers. Copper and tin were used to make weapons such as battle-axes, maces, bows and arrows, daggers, swords, and **scimitars.**

Warships

The first warship to be recorded appeared on the Nile. The early Egyptian ships were bundles of reeds lashed together and covered with pitch to make them watertight. From these early ships developed trading ships and warships built of wood and propelled by giant sails and oars. Large ships had twenty oars on each side. By the twelfth century B.C. planks were fitted to protect the rowers, and a small fighting platform on which archers stood was built high on the mast. A long pole called a ram was fitted to ships so that other ships could be rammed, splitting them or capsizing them.

Ivory handle of a flint knife depicting a river battle with boats and swimmers, from 3400 B.C..

Flint knife with animals carved on the handle, dated from 3400 B.C..

Battles

Battle scenes appear in paintings on the walls of Karnak, Abydos, and Abu Simbel. The **Palette of Narmer** (Narmer is thought to have been the first ruler of the first Egyptian dynasty) also depicts battle scenes. Tomb paintings show soldiers using scaling ladders and battering rams.

One battle of which we do know a great deal was the battle between the Egyptians and the Hittites at Kadesh in Syria, in about 1285 B.C..

The Egyptian army, led by Rameses II, fell into a trap at Kadesh when the Hittite army isolated the front section of the Egyptian army, which included Rameses. The Hittites, riding in 2,500 chariots with three men to a chariot, then descended on the second section of the Egyptian army, who rode in two-man chariots. A violent battle followed. Desperate fighting by the Egyptians ensured a draw, and the peace treaty is recorded both in Egyptian and Hittite.

Pictures, as well as accounts of the battle, an official record, a long poem carved into temple walls in Egypt and Nubia, and a papyrus copy of the poem have been found.

Egyptian Inventions and Special Skills

Shaduf

After the Nile flooded each year, the people learned to dam the water and direct it through canals and dikes to cultivate crops when needed. The shaduf was a cranelike device invented to lift the water from the canals or river. It consisted of a balanced beam with a bucket on one end to lift the water and a counterweight on the other.

Papyrus

This was a type of paper made from the reeds of the papyrus plant, which grew along the Nile. The fibers of the plant were laid side by side and a second layer placed at right angles. The layers were beaten, dampened, and pressed together, forming a sheet of paper when dried. The oldest known books are in the form of papyrus rolls.

Measuring

The Egyptians devised means of measuring and surveying. They needed to be able to measure the height of the Nile at each flood and reestablish the boundaries of farms and estates when the floods receded.

Pyramids

No other civilization built pyramids similar to those of the Egyptians or for the same reasons. The building of these pyramids show us how accurately Egyptian engineers, surveyors, mathematicians, and architects could calculate and measure. The Sphinx was built at the same time as the pyramids.

The Great Pyramid is 481 feet high (146.59 meters); each side is approximately 252 yards long (230 meters). The pyramid covers about 13 acres (54,000 square meters).

Ropemaking

Although ropemaking was not confined to Egypt, a high degree of skill was acquired by Egyptian ropemakers. Ropes had to be strong enough to support the huge stone blocks for building the pyramids and to haul the colossal statues. Ropes were made by intertwining strips of animal hides with flax fibers and fibers from the papyrus plant. Some ropes were plaited.

Roads

The first roads (causeways) to be made were in Egypt. Stones to build the temples and pyramids were hauled along these roads.

Loom

The earliest evidence of the use of a weaving loom dates back to 4400 B.C. Its use is illustrated on a pottery dish found at al-Badārī, in Egypt.

Hieroglyphics

This system of writing originally used characters in the form of pictures to represent a thing or an idea. Later, some of the signs evolved and were used to represent consonants, as in an alphabet. Because the Egyptians wrote so much, scholars have been able to understand aspects of Egyptian history and culture. The information contained on the Rosetta Stone greatly helped scholars in deciphering hieroglyphics.

Why the Civilization Declined

The Egyptian civilization began to decline at the time of Pharaoh Amenhotep IV. His disinterest in defending Egyptian lands by maintaining a strong, loyal army resulted in conquered countries being able to drive out the Egyptian army.

Amenhotep's interest was in a new religion which he ordered his people to adopt. He worshiped the god Aten, meaning "the disk of the sun," and even changed his name from Amenhotep to Akhenaten, meaning "It is well with Aten." He built a new capital, Akhetaten, "Horizon of Aten," and lived there with his family. He forbade the worship of old gods. This confused the people, made them resentful and fearful, and eventually led to civil unrest. Upon his death, the people returned to the worship of their old gods and the priests, fearful these events could happen again, became even more powerful under his successor, Tutankhamon.

Later, Seti I, Rameses II, and successors regained Egyptian lands and defended the country. From the seventh century B.C. on, Egypt was continually invaded and controlled by Assyrians, Babylonians, Persians, Greeks, and Romans.

The inventions and originality that helped Egypt to become self-sufficient and powerful began to decline. Political and administrative control weakened and the rigidity of cultural institutions prevented the Egyptians from responding to new threats and challenges. Education and intellectual life lagged behind developments in other countries. Their armies were largely composed of mercenary soldiers in later years. Many of these soldiers were foreign slaves, not Egyptians loyal to the pharaoh, and therefore were more easily defeated.

Under the Greeks, the Greek and Egyptian civilizations merged, and the days of pure Egyptian civilization came to an end.

Opposite: a modern Egyptian. The Temple of Karnak at Luxor is in the background.

Left: a modern Egyptian boy on a mule.

Glossary

Amulet A protective charm worn to ward off evil spirits.

Annals Historical records that identified major events and floods.

Armor Protective covering of metal or leather worn over other clothes by soldiers in battle to protect the wearer from being wounded by an enemy weapon.

Artifacts Objects made by people, including tools, such as an ax, knife blades, grinding stones, and vessels of pottery, metal, or stone.

Chariot A two-wheeled vehicle used in war, pulled by a horse or other animal.

Chironomy A system of hand signals used by singers to direct instrumentalists.

Cyclone A pressure system moving in a circular direction which brings strong winds and heavy rain in a short time.

Demotic script A form of writing invented by the Egyptians for use on documents.

Embalming Treating a corpse with natron, spices, perfumes, and linen strips to try to preserve its appearance and prevent decay.

Emmer A form of wheat grown in early times in countries around the Mediterranean. It is different in appearance from wheat grown on farms in most places today.

Flax A slender plant with narrow, pointed leaves and blue flowers. The fiber of this plant is manufactured into yarn or thread which is woven into linen or used to make rope.

Frieze A band carved or printed on a wall, depicting historical events and scenes of daily life.

Hieroglyphics An Egyptian writing system of pictures which had a standard meaning. This writing was carved into stone or other hard surfaces.

Indigo A dark blue vat dye obtained from plants such as indigo.

Largesse To bestow or apportion gifts or money. In Egyptian times, animals and seed belonging to the landlord would be apportioned to the tenant farmers.

Lentils Small edible seeds that can be kept in a dried state and, later, when soaked in water, become soft and are delicious and healthful to eat.

Madder A moderate to strong red dye obtained from the root of the Eurasian madder plant.

Mantle A loose, sleeveless garment worn over other clothes.

Millennium A period of a thousand years.

Mummy A dead body of a human being or animal that was preserved by the Egyptian process of embalming.

Palette of Narmer A carved slate tablet thought to have been used for mixing cosmetics and belonging to the Egyptian king Narmer. There are many intricate carvings on both sides of the palette depicting scenes of Egyptian life at that time.

Papyrus A form of paper manufactured in Egypt from the fiber of the stem of the papyrus reed, which grew in the Nile Valley. Writing on papyrus was done with a reed pen dipped in ink. Plural *papyri*.

Pharaoh The title given to the king of Egypt.

Pitch A dark substance made from wood sap and resins, and used to cover ships' hulls to make them watertight.

Plat A plan or map of land or buildings.

Prehistoric Belonging to a period before that of recorded (written) history.

Rosetta Stone A stone found in Egypt in the late eighteenth century that has three different scripts: hieroglyphic, demotic, and Greek. The information on this stone has enabled scholars to decipher the Egyptian language and script.

Scimitar A curved single-edged sword.

Scribe One who wrote or copied documents, letters, and other manuscripts.

Shaduf A cranelike device used for raising water from a canal or river in Egypt. It consisted of a long beam with a bucket on one end and a counterweight on the other.

Silt Fine sand and earth carried by running water from high land of the river and deposited as thick mud or sediment on low-lying areas. It provides fertile land for crops.

Sphinx An imaginary creature with the head of a person and the body of a lion.

Tenant farmer One who farms land rented from another. In Egyptian times the land (estate) was owned by the landlord, king, or temple, who directed the work of the farm and the tenant farmers.

Terracotta A glazed or unglazed fired earthenware; a brownish-orange color.

Vizier The highest official appointed by the pharaoh, to whom considerable power was given.

The Egyptians: Some Famous People and Places

NEFERTITI

Nefertiti was queen of Egypt and wife of King Akhenaten, who ruled from 1379 to 1362 B.C. She supported her husband's new religion, the worship of the sun god Aten. It is believed that Nefertiti was an Asian princess from Mit Anni. In the twelfth year of her husband's reign, Nefertiti either died or retired from public life, as her eldest daughter appears to have taken over her royal duties. Objects belonging to the queen have been found in Amarna in the north, so quite possibly this is where she retired. Her tomb has not been found.

TUTANKHAMON

Tutankhamon was king of Egypt from 1361 to 1352 B.C. He changed his name from Tutankhaten to Tutankhamon. He moved his residence to Memphis, near present-day Cairo, and restored his father's palace at Thebes. He also restored other temples, and recognized the old Egyptian gods. He died unexpectedly at 18 years of age, and Ay, who succeeded him, married his widow.

His tomb was discovered in 1922. Because the tomb had remained hidden, it had escaped being robbed. Tutankhamon's mummy lay within a nest of three coffins, the outer two of gold-covered wood, and the inner coffin of solid gold. The burial rooms were crammed with precious jewels, chariots, and furniture.

RAMESEUM

Rameseum is the ruined funeral temple of Rameses II, who ruled from 1304 to 1237 B.C. It was built on the west bank of the Nile at Thebes in Upper Egypt. The temple was dedicated to the god Amon and contained a huge statue (now only a fragment) of Rameses II, and figures of the king as Osiris. The walls of the temple were decorated with reliefs, and include the Battle of Kadesh, scenes of the king's wars against the Syrians, and the Festival of Min, the harvest god. Around the temple are remains of mud bricks and vaulted storerooms, probably like those built by the Israelites in northern Egypt just before the Exodus.

HATSHEPSUT

Hatshepsut was queen of Egypt, and ruled in her own right from 1503 to 1482 B.C. as pharaoh. She adopted a Horus name and wore the full regalia of a pharaoh, including a false beard, which all kings wore traditionally. She sent an expedition by sea to the African coast, and had gold, ebony, animal skins, baboons, and processed myrrh as well as live myrrh trees brought back to Egypt. She undertook an extensive building program to honor the god Amon-Re and restored many damaged buildings and monuments. Her unique funeral monument, the temple at Deir al-Bahri, records the major events of her reign.

THEBES

Thebes was an ancient Egyptian city located on the banks of the Nile. It was important during the Middle Kingdom and the New Kingdom. Thebes was originally called Wase or Wa'se, from the sacred *was*, meaning scepter. The main part of the city was on the east bank, while on the west bank was the "city of the dead," which held mortuary temples, houses of the priests, soldiers, craftsmen, and laborers.

The earliest monuments which survive at Thebes date from the eleventh dynasty (2133 to 1911 B.C.). Thebes became the royal capital and was called Nowe or Nuwe, "the city of Amon," after the chief god. Many temples and palaces were built at Thebes, including the temples of Karnak and Luxor. During the reign of Amenhotep III, great quantities of wealth, in the form of tributes from foreign lands, were sent to Thebes. Rameses III donated slaves and estates to the temples.

By about 1211 B.C., Thebes began to decline and much of its treasure was plundered.

The Nubian pharaohs made Thebes their capital, and the city was famous throughout the Greek world. The Greeks referred to it as the "hundred-gated Thebes."

ELEPHANTINE

Elephantine is the modern Greek name for the old Egyptian city of Yeb (Elephant Town) on an island in the Nile. During the nineteenth and eighteenth dynasties, pharaohs built a temple to Khnum, the ram god, to his consort Sati, and to Anuket, the goddess of Sehel. In early times, Elephantine was located at the first cataract, where a ridge of granite rises in the riverbed preventing ships and boats from passing.

SETI I

Seti I was an Egyptian king of the nineteenth dynasty, and father of Rameses II. Seti is recognized by many scholars as the greatest king of the nineteenth dynasty. He regained much prestige and power for Egypt, which had been lost during the eighteenth dynasty. He helped build the great temple at Karnak as well as his own mortuary temple at Abydos. Seti's burial chamber is the finest in the Valley of the Tombs of Kings, at Thebes.

CHEOPS

Cheops is the Greek name for Khufu, king of Egypt's fourth dynasty. He was regarded as a wise ruler. During his reign, the Great Pyramid at Giza was built. This was the largest single building ever erected. Khufu was married four times, first to Merityetes. His second queen is not known. His third wife was Henutsen, and his fourth wife was Nefert-kau. His wives are buried in three small pyramids beside his own Great Pyramid.

An ivory statue of Khufu is in the Museum in Cairo.

NECTANEBO II

Nectanebo II was the last native Egyptian pharaoh, whose death in 343 B.C. marked the end of the thirtieth dynasty. He was also called Nektharheb II or Nekhtharehbe II. His most powerful enemy was King Artaxerxes III Ochus, the Persian king, who invaded and took control of Egypt.

MANETHO

Manetho was an Egyptian priest who lived in the third century B.C. He was also a writer, and he wrote a history of Egypt in Greek. This history has not survived except for some fragments quoted in other works. It was Manetho who divided the rulers of Egypt into thirty dynasties, and this is still accepted by modern scholars.

Index